Risk Management:
A Guide to Good Practice

Acknowledgements

This guide has been prepared by CIMA's Fraud and Risk Management Working Group, which was established to look at ways of helping management accountants to be more effective in countering fraud and managing risk in their organisations.

The Working Group comprises:

David Cafferty, ACMA CFE, Matson Driscoll & Damico (Chair)
Lanre Amao, Head of Audit, ActionAid
Denis Day, Director of Internal Audit, City University
Kay Dickinson, Director of Finance and Resources, Sector Skills Development Agency
Anthony Dodd, Senior Risk Manager, Royal Mail Group plc
Mike Frankl, Director of Finance, Reform Synagogues of Great Britain
Roy Katzenberg, Assistant Director, Forensic Group, Ernst & Young LLP
Peter Ludlow, IT Development Manager, Costain Ltd
Richard Meade, Director of Chichester Diocesan Housing Association and of VETAID
Peter Wishart, formerly Financial Manager, Xerox Ltd

with Judy Finn, Project Manager, CIMA Technical Services

The group would like to thank the many colleagues of Working Group members and Bill Connell, Director of Risk Management, BOC Group who have assisted with the writing of this guide.

Further copies of this guide can be purchased from CIMA Publishing and is also available to CIMA members on the internet at: www.cimaglobal.com

About CIMA

Founded on the collective knowledge and experience of a professional body entirely focused on management accounting, CIMA (The Chartered Institute of Management Accountants) is one of the world's leading accounting bodies with ten offices worldwide, over 133,000 members and students in 150 countries. CIMA is the only institute whose sole focus is to provide training and professional qualifications for accountants working in business and the public sector. The CIMA perspective is directed towards all the key issues that face many finance directors irrespective of the size of the business or the sector. This strong business focus is grounded in the CIMA syllabus.

Contents

Appendices

Index

'When anyone asks me how I can describe my experience of nearly forty years at sea, I merely say uneventful. Of course, there have been winter gales and storms and fog and the like, but in all my experience I have never been in an accident of any sort worth speaking about. I have seen but one vessel in distress in all my years at sea...I never saw a wreck and have never been wrecked, nor was I ever in any predicament that threatened to end in disaster of any sort.'

Capt. E. J. Smith, later Captain of RMS Titanic

Introduction

Introduction

The traditional one-dimensional view of risk is no longer sustainable. Shareholder and social value depend much on other non-financial factors such as leadership, culture, employee commitment, customer loyalty and reputation. These 'soft' factors need to be protected and nurtured within a robust risk management framework. As a consequence risk management is moving higher up the agenda for all organisations.

Uncertainty has always been a part of business, no more so than at the present time. However, organisations are beginning to recognise that effective management of the resultant risks can make an important contribution to business improvement. In addition, there is external pressure on organisations to improve all aspects of governance. For example, McKinsey & Company's 'Global Investor Opinion Survey on Corporate Governance' (2002) showed that an overwhelming majority of institutional investors are prepared to pay a significant premium for companies exhibiting high governance standards.

As a result, risk management is evolving from a reactive response to crisis or a 'tick-box' exercise into a proactive activity which forms a key part of the strategic management process. By offering strategic solutions throughout the organisation, risk management can provide a tool to minimise the impact of adverse events and enhance the returns from new opportunities. Integrated risk management (often referred to as 'Enterprise Risk Management' (ERM)), which encompasses the whole organisation and sees risks as opportunities to be grasped as much as hazards, is being seen as essential for achieving and maintaining competitive advantage.

Organisations across the world are beginning to implement ERM systems. However, most are some way from completing the journey. Recent research carried out by the Economist Intelligence Unit of 40 major companies in North America, Europe and Asia found that although 41 per cent of companies had adopted ERM, only 15 per cent aggregate risk across their entire organisation.

Management accountants, whose professional training includes the analysis of information and systems, performance and strategic management, can have a significant role to play in developing and implementing risk management and internal control systems within their organisations. As the role of finance managers evolves they are increasingly taking responsibility for driving the organisation's risk management either individually or as part of a multidisciplinary group.

This guide has been written with such finance managers in mind, particularly those who have little or no prior experience of risk management and find themselves responsible for, or involved in, all or part of their organisation's approach to risk management. This guide should also be read by line managers seeking to gain deeper insight into ensuring an effective risk management approach and who desire risk to become an everyday part of their management process.

We hope that it will also be of use to any organisation wanting to implement an approach to risk management which can contribute to improved competitive advantage and increase shareholder value. It provides an overview of risk management accompanied by practical examples that any organisation can use or adapt. These examples are not intended to be prescriptive or to apply directly to all organisations, but to provoke thought and provide ideas. However, the principles contained in this guide do apply to all organisations.

This guide is complemented by the new theme booklet from the Financial and Management Accounting Committee (FMAC) of the International Federation of Accountants (IFAC) and CIMA. IFAC explores emerging trends and seeks to represent contemporary best practice in the domain of the professional accountant in business. The booklet, entitled *Managing Risk to Enhance Stakeholder Value,* provides candid views on various aspects of risk management from finance professionals and others working in business.

Further copies of both these publications can be obtained from CIMA Publishing.

What is Risk Management?

Risks are the opportunities and dangers associated with uncertain future events. There is risk in any situation where there is a possibility of more than one outcome. If the outcome is certain there is no risk. The existence of risk leads to uncertainty, but the level of uncertainty will vary both with knowledge and attitude. Risks may not even be recognised, but a lack of recognition does not alter their existence.

For an organisation, risks are potential events that could influence the achievement of the organisation's objectives. Risk management is the process of understanding the nature of such events and making positive plans to mitigate them where they represent threats or to take advantage where they represent opportunities.

1.1 Why manage risk?

There are numerous and well-documented disasters caused by poor risk management. One of the most well-known examples has to be that of the Titanic, which set sail in 1912 across the treacherous waters of the North Atlantic with only sufficient lifeboats for half the passengers aboard (though more than required by the law of the time). No provision had been made for the other passengers aboard, nor was the crew adequately prepared or able to respond to the iceberg warnings. Following the tragedy, many new regulations were implemented. For example, all ships were required to carry enough lifeboats for all passengers and crew, the universal distress call 'SOS' was introduced and a 24-hour radio watch was made compulsory.

1.1.1 No immunity from risk

No business is immune from risks. Many companies, including household names, have suffered from unforeseen events that have had a significant effect on their reputation and balance sheet. In 1990 regulators in the US discovered that Perrier bottled water was contaminated with benzene. The company responded quickly by recalling all bottles in North America stating that they believed the contamination could be traced to a fluid containing benzene that was being used on the bottling line for bottles intended for that market. Then benzene was found by officials from other countries, which led to a world-wide recall and an embarrassed source at Perrier altering its original explanation. The new story was that benzene was naturally present in carbon dioxide and should have been filtered out before the water was bottled. It took years for sales of Perrier water in North Amercia to recover.

Case study 1:
Why think about risk? – the Hoover experience

Hoover executives learnt a hard lesson when poor risk management led to a company whose name had become synonymous with vacuum cleaners becoming better known for its marketing misjudgement.

In 1992, under pressure from the company's US parent to improve sales and profits, senior executives endorsed a promotion offering two free return air tickets to Europe if customers spent £100 or more on a new Hoover product. However, following the success of this promotion, they agreed to extend it to a promise of return tickets to America. These tickets were worth far more than the value of the product, and the upside for customers was worth far more than the downside of buying a machine they didn't really need. Hoover sales rocketed, but as more and more tickets were claimed it soon became clear that the idea had gone further than Hoover's management ever anticipated.

Some businesses exploited Hoover's embarrassment by offering a free Hoover complete with the free ticket offer in return for purchase of their own goods. As people bought new machines they didn't really need – even a loss on the purchase was acceptable in return for the free tickets – a flourishing second-hand market grew up in vacuum cleaners which damaged the business the promotion was supposed to help. The US owners of the company had to set aside millions of dollars to cover the costs and set up a task force to handle the claims. Thousands of people didn't get the flights they requested as Hoover cited small print limiting availability, leading to a customer relations nightmare and many law suits.

So, why did it happen? Under pressure to perform, managers placed too much weight on the sales volumes expected from the offer and pursued the upside without paying sufficient attention to what could go wrong. Customers, however, did make an assessment of the risks and opportunities for them, and won.

Based on material from Dembo, R and Freeman, A (1998),
Seeing Tomorrow – Rewriting the Rules of Risk, John Wiley and Sons, Inc.

1.1.2 The impact of external events

Events can have far-reaching consequences beyond those for the individuals directly involved as seen in the continuing impact of the events of September 11th 2001. Not only were many lives lost and billions of dollars worth of damage caused, but some of the indirect effects are increased insurance premiums as insurers try to recoup some of the losses, increased air fares, longer check-ins, tighter security at airports, and the impact of the ongoing 'war on terrorism'. The event's impact on the world's stock markets will be felt by anyone with a pension, endowment policy or investments generally thought of as low-risk.

1.1.3 The business environment

The environment in which businesses operate is also changing. Developments such as e-business and globalisation mean organisations need to respond faster to change and are therefore exposed to a wide range of different risks. One such example is the increased risk of fraud, which we all pay for indirectly through bank charges and other costs. Additionally, expectations of stakeholders and the public have risen and organisations are expected to show more responsibility and have well-developed risk management strategies.

1.1.4 Corporate governance and risk management

In recent years, the issue of corporate governance and how to manage risk has been a major area for concern in many countries. In an early example, in the US, the Treadway Commission's 'Report on Fraudulent Financial Reporting' (1987) confirmed the role and status of audit committees in providing independent oversight of the organisation's governance and risk management. Subsequently the Securities and Exchange Commission (SEC) introduced the requirement that all SEC-regulated companies should have an audit committee with a majority of non-executive directors. A sub-group of the Treadway Commission then developed a framework for internal control, providing detailed criteria for management to assess internal control systems and how to report publicly on internal control.

In the UK, Listed Companies now have to meet the requirements of the Combined Code of Corporate Governance which calls for Boards to establish systems of internal control and to review the effectiveness of these systems on a regular basis. Subsequently, the Turnbull Committee was set up to issue guidance to directors on how they should assess and report on their review of this effectiveness. The Committee highlighted that establishing risk management practices, which should be embedded in the operations of an organisation and form part of its culture, is key to effective internal control systems. Organisations in most other sectors of the economy are also required to report on risk management. However, even if it is not mandatory it is an activity that every organisation should undertake.

Case study 2: Risk management isn't just for businesses
Example: the Galapagos National Park

The Galapagos National Park is one of the world's most important ecological sites, largely because it has been virtually isolated from man's intervention. However, in January 2001 the archipelago hit the international headlines when the tanker Jessica ran aground as it approached San Cristobal Island.

Even before she left port, the Jessica was in a poor state, both electronically and mechanically, and her hull was worn and rusty. Her captain was unfamiliar with Galapagos waters, had no local charts and did not have the appropriate qualifications or experience to command such a vessel. To compound matters the Jessica appears not to have been insured.

For four days after the tanker went aground, the owners of the cargo, the state-owned company Petroecuador, would not allow any attempt to remove the fuel. Help was on hand from the US Coast Guard's Gulf Coast Oil Spill Strike Force but this was stalled because the Government of Ecuador would not cover the costs of the Coast Guard. Eventually they reached an agreement but only after the tanker's hull had breached.

Fortunately, favourable weather averted what could have been an appalling environmental disaster, but action needs to be taken to avoid a different outcome next time around. Ecological monitoring of potentially affected sites and species is likely to continue for two to three years. Complementary work is being done to improve the regulatory framework in order to prevent environmental disasters of all kinds. Contingency plans are being prepared for future incidents.

The total cost of mitigation and clean-up operations, plus the forthcoming evaluation, monitoring, and contingency planning, will run into millions of dollars.

Based on material from *Galapagos News*, Summer 2001, published by the Galapagos Conservation Trust.

1.2 The upside of risk management

The emphasis of this chapter has so far been on loss prevention. Avoiding hazards, minimising the likelihood of failure and protecting business are at the heart of most organisations' risk management strategies. However, recently organisations have begun to view risk from a different perspective. Risks are being seen increasingly in terms of opportunities to be seized.

The concept of the link between risk and return is a familiar one, and investors view risk as worthwhile if the associated return is high enough. For example, shrewd investors who took risks in the early days of dot.com businesses made large profits before pulling out of the market in advance of the crash.

Organisations are beginning to apply this to their risk management practices, broadening their view of risk to encompass the management of opportunities and the need to increase the likelihood of positive outcomes in order to maximise returns. This is not to say that organisations have not managed risks in the past, but that the emphasis is changing. Risk management is becoming part of the business strategy aimed at enhancing performance by realising the rewards associated with those risks. Exposing the organisation to more uncertainty in conjunction with effective risk management can be critical to improving a company's performance.

Effective risk management can have a positive effect on the balance sheet by protecting profit margins and even improving them. The benefits will depend on how risk management is implemented; the most important are outlined below.

- *Taking advantage of new opportunities* can be done most successfully if the organisation identifies and understands the associated risks and develops an appropriate response.
- *Better communications* as risk management becomes part of the culture – it demands an organisation-wide approach and a common language to be effective.
- *Promotion of continuous improvement* will be a result of the risk management cycle which includes a continual review of what went wrong and the organisation's response.
- *A focus for internal audit* based, not on the traditional cyclical programme, but on the priorities resulting from the risk management

programme. This can also lead to a decrease in cost. A major organisation in the UK reduced its internal audit staffing by three-quarters by focusing on the key priorities rather than every individual activity.

- *Fewer shocks and surprises* as an organisation becomes better at forecasting risks and likely outcomes from uncertainty, and develops an increased ability to prevent major losses.
- *Reassurance for stakeholders* whose expectations have increased and who are looking for evidence of good risk management practices.
- *Enhanced shareholder value* as the rewards from opportunities are realised.
- *Increased likelihood of objectives being achieved* as the discipline of risk management ensures that potential problems are identified and associated losses minimised.

The Risk Management Process

2.1 An integrated approach to risk management

Evidence suggests that historically, risk management has been a peripheral activity in many organisations. Fragmented and unstructured, it has often concentrated on risks at the operational level, with strategic risks ignored or considered on an ad-hoc basis. This form of risk management tends to be reactive rather than proactive, and largely concerned with minimising loss rather than taking advantage of opportunities.

As risk management began to develop, large organisations often followed a decentralised approach with each department or business unit developing its own strategy and using different tools and techniques. This is often the case where business units face different risk factors from one unit to the next or where units operate independently. While this approach is better than that described above, it has disadvantages:

- different approaches are used for common risks facing all departments;
- there is little or no consideration of risk at an aggregated level;
- it is difficult for experience and practice to be shared;
- the overall cost of risk management is likely to be higher due to duplication;
- risks affecting the whole organisation may be missed.

The drive to improve corporate governance and the associated responsibility for boards of companies has raised the profile of risk management and led organisations to change their approach.

There is also growing recognition that the management of risks is key to the future health and survival of organisations and therefore of central strategic importance. Well-publicised failures of large companies due to unrecognised risks at a strategic level have also contributed. It is now generally recognised that best practice is an integrated, holistic approach (often referred to as Enterprise Risk Management, or ERM) where risk management forms part of the strategic business management and is implemented on an organisation-wide basis. Where it is most effective, risk management becomes an integral part of the culture of the organisation and embedded in its processes.

When risk management is part of the strategic planning cycle of an organisation, the organisation's objectives provide the context and parameters within which risks are managed. The organisation's policies will define the criteria used for deciding whether a given risk is acceptable or not and help to shape the strategies for responding to risks. Advantages of integrated risk management are that:

- the risk profile of the entire organisation will be considered;
- risk management is more likely to be seen as everyone's responsibility;
- risk management will be based on overall strategic objectives and focused on key risks and opportunities that contribute to achieving those objectives;
- it will support the strategic planning of the business;
- experience and practice can be shared across the business;
- a common set of tools and techniques will be used in different departments and business units;
- inter-departmental communication will be improved;
- risk management can become part of the culture of the organisation and embedded into all its processes and activities.

The following diagram, taken from CBI and KPMG, *Managing Business Risk*, 2001, Caspian Publishing and KPMG, illustrates the way in which the risk management strategy should be aligned with the organisational strategy, its vision, mission, objectives and initiatives for growth and development.

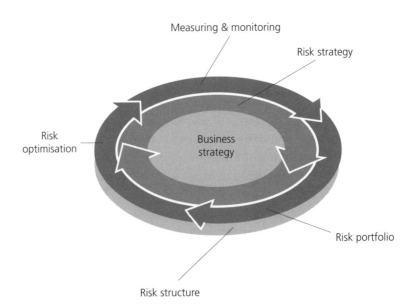

2.2 The process: the risk management cycle

The implementation of integrated risk management demands a systematic approach. One such approach, the risk management cycle, is an iterative process of identifying risks, assessing their impact, and prioritising actions to control and reduce risks.

The following diagram illustrates the steps in the risk management cycle (adapted from *Managing the Risk of Fraud – A Guide for Managers*, HM Treasury, 1997). Each of these steps will be considered in more detail in the following chapters of the guide. Any organisation implementing integrated risk management will need to go through all of these steps, but the detail of the actions taken will vary depending on the organisation – for example a small business is unlikely to need to follow the steps in such a formal way.

The risk management cycle

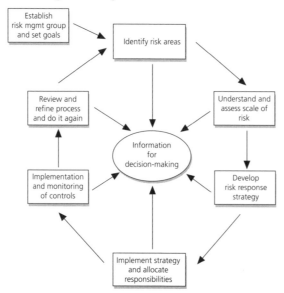

2.2.1 Establish a risk management group and set goals

A risk management group may be established to facilitate and co-ordinate the overall process. The group's objective would be to provide advice, educate the organisation about and raise awareness of risk management and related issues. The exact composition of the group will be dependent on the organisation's characteristics, but a multi-disciplinary group is likely to be the most effective.

2.2.2 Identify risk areas

Each risk in the overall risk model should be explored to identify how it potentially evolves through the organisation. It is important to ensure that the risks are carefully defined and explained to facilitate further analysis.

2.2.3 Understand and assess the scale of risk

Once risks have been identified, an assessment of the possible impact and likelihood of occurrence should be carried out using consistent parameters that will enable the risks to be prioritised. The risk assessment should not simply take account of the financial impact but also consider its impact on the organisation's viability and reputation, and recognise the political and commercial sensitivities involved.

2.2.4 Develop a risk response strategy

Once the risks have been identified and assessed, strategies to deal with each risk that has been identified can be developed by line managers, with guidance from the Risk Management Group.

2.2.5 Implement the strategy and allocate responsibilities

The chosen strategy should be agreed with and communicated to those identified as responsible for its implementation.

2.2.6 Implement and monitor suggested controls

The chosen strategy may require the implementation of new controls or the modification of existing controls. Businesses are dynamic and the controls that are in place will need to be monitored to assess whether or not they are succeeding in their objectives.

2.2.7 Do it again

All the above processes must form part of an iterative cycle where risk management is being continually reviewed and developed. As this cycle continues, risk management can become increasingly embedded in the organisation so that it really becomes part of everyone's job.

2.2.8 Information for decision making

Risk management is a key part of the organisation's decision-making process. At all stages in the risk management cycle information is gathered which should be fed into the decision-making mechanisms.

Organisations will be at different stages in the development of their approach to risk management. The flowchart in Appendix 2 can be used to help identify which stage an organisation is at and what actions need to be taken to develop risk management further.

An article in the FMAC/CIMA theme booklet considers how the BOC Group manages risk within the context of its strategy.

Identifying and Analysing Risks

As has already been explained, the first stage in the process of establishing risk management is to identify the key risk areas facing the organisation. There is a broad range of risks facing any organisation; at many levels these risks can be generic and apply to all organisations, or be specific to a particular sector or organisation. Risks may also be 'strategic' in that they relate directly to the overall objectives of the organisation, such as competition, or at an operational level where they concern activities carried out within the organisation. They may affect all areas of an organisation or be localised applying only to specific units, projects or processes. Many risks will impact on one another or have consequences for apparently unconnected areas of an organisation. The process of identifying, quantifying and prioritising risks is often referred to as 'risk mapping'.

3.1 Sources of risk

Organisations face a range of risks from various sources. Understanding the different risks and where they may arise will help organisations to manage them. Some risks are 'organisational', in that they occur within an organisation and are a function of an organisation's operations and under its control. An organisation can manage such risks once they have been identified. 'Global risks', that do not relate specifically to an organisation and its business, such as climate change or war are out of the organisation's control but an organisation can still prepare a response. Between these two extremes are a range of risks that can be influenced by the organisation, if not controlled.

3.2 Different types of risk

3.2.1 Classifying risks

It is helpful to consider risks as falling into certain categories. One way of breaking down risks is into operational, financial and environmental risks. Some risks may fall into more than one category.

Operational risks

These relate to the activities carried out within an organisation. They may arise from the structure or systems within the organisation, its people, products or its processes.

Examples are:

- business interruption;
- errors or omissions by employees;
- product design failures;
- systems security;
- fraud;
- loss of systems or locations;
- loss of key people;
- poor quality supplies;
- termination of contracts by suppliers.

Financial risks

Financial risks, relating to the financial operation of a company's business, are often outside an organisation's control but can be influenced by its actions. Examples are:

- credit risk;
- liquidity risks;
- currency risks;
- cash-flow risks.

Environmental risks

Environmental risks arise from forces in the political, economic, social and financial environment over which an organisation has little influence. Examples of environmental risks are:

- political decisions;
- climate change;
- regulation;
- natural disasters;
- loss of business;
- competition;
- economic slowdown;
- stock market fluctuations.

3.2.2 Organisational risks

A key group of risks that are often forgotten or underestimated are the softer, organisational issues, for example those relating to the behaviour of individuals and groups within the organisation. These are of particular importance for organisations going through major change, where the support and co-operation of staff is key to the success of the change programme. Failure to identify and manage risks such as a refusal by a team to work in a different way can lead to disaster. Such risks are often the hardest to deal with but must be recognised and included in any risk mapping exercise.

3.2.3 Reputational risks

There is growing interest in the idea of 'reputational' risk as a distinct type of risk, particularly following well-publicised failures such as that of Enron and WorldCom that have had a major impact on the reputations of the accounting profession and Andersen in particular. However, it could be argued that damage to an organisation's reputation is a result of a failure to manage other risks, rather than being a specific category in itself. Steve Marshall, former CEO of Railtrack, and Steve Harvey, Director of People, Profit and Culture at Microsoft, share their insight and provide interesting views on the issues around managing reputation in the FMAC/CIMA theme booklet.

An example of risk classification as used by a large UK service business

Appendix 3 shows the range of risks facing a telecommunications business.

3.3 Identifying risks

In order for the risk identification process to provide a sound foundation for an effective risk management process, it must be comprehensive and include risks at all levels. An area that has not been covered could be the one to cost the organisation dearly when the unforeseen event occurs. Risks at an individual level must be taken into account even if they are later aggregated to enable management of the risks. In addition, the process must be iterative – the environment in which the organisation operates is continually changing and new risks will emerge, whilst others decline in importance. The risk identification process must include not only existing risks, but also allow for emerging risks – those that do not currently impact on the business but could do in the future.

The risks facing an organisation will vary according to the business and environment within which it operates. The risk identification process must be carried out in the context of the nature of the business and the culture within the organisation. It also needs to take account of the constraints within which the organisation operates, whether internal structures and policies or external requirements from government or stakeholders. A good understanding of all these factors is critical if the risks facing the organisation are to be correctly identified.

3.3.1 Top-down or bottom-up?

Some organisations have developed a top-down approach to risk identification, by looking at the organisation from a corporate perspective. This may involve the use of publicly available information and include brainstorming sessions and interviews with key individuals at a senior level in the organisation. Advantages of this approach are that:

- It is likely to take into account and reflect the strategic objectives of the organisation.
- It will reflect external influences affecting the whole organisation.

- The participants are likely to have a breadth of experience of the organisation and possibly of other organisations.
- Risks will be identified at an organisation-wide level.

Other organisations have adopted a bottom-up approach. This involves identifying risks at an individual department level that are then combined to provide an analysis at an aggregate level. Advantages of the bottom-up approach are that:

- Employees throughout the organisation are involved in the process that helps to establish risk awareness throughout the organisation.
- It provides a framework for risk management at a devolved level.
- It will ensure the identification of risks specific to departments that might otherwise be missed.
- It provides a different perspective on risks from those most closely involved in the processes.

Organisations have tended to use one approach rather than the other. However, the most effective method of identifying risks is to use a combination of both approaches as best fits the organisation. For example, one UK business looks at risks both top-down from a corporate level and then at key processes cutting across business units. These processes are in turn examined from both a corporate perspective and then at the business unit level. Whatever approach is taken, it must allow all possible risk areas and interrelationships between them to be included.

3.3.2 Tools and techniques for identifying risks

There are many tools and techniques that can be used to identify risks. Some of the most important are described below.

- *Brainstorming* can be very useful as a means of generating raw information about perceived risks for further analysis, and can be used at different levels within the organisation. As with any brainstorming exercise, it is important that the ideas are not evaluated during the brainstorming process in order to ensure that the flow of ideas is maintained.
- *Workshops with employees* can provide useful insights into risks and attitudes throughout the organisation. The perception of dif-

ferent groups of employees very often differs from that of the board. In addition, certain risks that may seem insignificant to members of senior management may become more important when associated with individuals who are charged with operational delivery. These activities also help to embed risk management in the processes of the organisation.

- *Dialogues with stakeholders* form a useful part of a top-down process, both in identifying risks and understanding the likely impact.
- *Benchmarking, either internal or external* can provide useful input where information is available either about their own risk analysis or where problems have arisen and been documented. Some useful sources of benchmarks are industry journals and surveys and internal benchmarking between divisions within the organisation itself.
- *Checklists* can be used to ensure that risk areas are not missed. These may be general or industry-specific and can often be found in books on risk management.

3.4 Assessing the scale of risk

Once risks have been identified, risk mapping requires an assessment of possible impact and corresponding likelihood of occurrence. Estimates should be made using consistent parameters that will enable the development of a prioritised risk analysis. At the planning stage management should agree on the most appropriate definition and number of categories to be used when assessing both likelihood and impact.

The assessment of the impact of the risk should not simply take account of the financial impact but should also consider any impact on the organisation's viability and reputation, as well as recognise the political and commercial sensitivities involved. The analysis can be either qualitative or quantitative, but should be consistent to allow for comparison and trend analysis. The qualitative approach usually involves grading risks in high, medium and low categories.

3.4.1 Impact

Assessing the potential impact of a particular risk may be complicated by the fact that a range of possible outcomes may exist or that the risk may occur a number of times in a given period of time. The organisation should anticipate such outcomes and adopt a consistent approach that could, for example, estimate a worst-case scenario over a twelve-month time period.

3.4.2 Likelihood of occurrence

The likelihood of a risk occurring should be assessed on a gross, a net and a target basis.

A 'gross basis' assesses the inherent likelihood of the event occurring in the absence of any processes that the organisation may have in place to reduce the likelihood.

A 'net basis' assesses the likelihood, taking into account current conditions and processes to mitigate the chance of the event occurring.

The 'target likelihood' of a risk occurring reflects the risk appetite of the organisation. Where the net likelihood and the target likelihood for a particular risk differ, this would indicate the need to alter the risk profile accordingly.

It is common practice to assess likelihood in terms of:

- high – probable;
- moderate – possible; or
- low – remote.

Once an assessment of the likelihood and consequences of risks has been made, a risk matrix (often referred to as 'the risk map') can be drawn up. A risk map or matrix is a means of displaying together all the risks facing the organisation in terms of their likelihood and impact. The use of a risk map enables the organisation to identify different categories of risk that require different responses. For example risks with a high impact and high likelihood will demand further investigation and an active response, whilst those of low likelihood and low impact will be lower priorities.

An example of a risk map is shown in Appendix 4.

3.4.3 Developing a risk portfolio

It would be an unmanageable task to respond to each individual risk separately. For this reason organisations develop a risk portfolio. This is a technique for grouping or categorising risks to give a view of the total risk exposure, identify the links between risks and draw out the key risks facing the business. Attention can then be focused on a smaller number of consolidated risk groups rather than a large number of individual risks.

3.4.4 Tools and techniques for assessing risks

Once the most significant risks have been identified, a more detailed analysis can be carried out to quantify their impact on the organisation. Some of the tools available are described below:

- *Information gathering* from existing management reports and discussions with managers can provide useful data about the possible impact of risks.
- *Scenario planning* involves developing alternative hypothetical views of possible future outcomes that would not otherwise be considered. These scenarios are generally developed through a series of wide-ranging discussions and interviews with decision-makers. Scenario planning can be used to challenge existing assumptions and can also improve decision-makers' understanding of risk.
- *Computer simulations* can be used to estimate the outcomes and their probabilities by running the model repeatedly. In the case of one such model, the Monte Carlo simulation, the uncertainties in a project are quantified using probability distributions, which are sampled by the computer to generate a large range of scenarios. These scenarios are then evaluated. The model provides information on the wide range of possible outcomes from the project and their probabilities.
- *Decision trees* can be used to map stages in a project and the possible uncertainties or decisions at each stage. By estimating the probabilities of each uncertainty and the likely cashflows, an evaluation can be made of each final outcome, its likelihood and an expected value for the whole project.
- *Sensitivity analysis* is used to determine how sensitive an outcome is to changes in the factors affecting it. This is done by

changing the values of those factors and observing the effect on the outcome.

- *Real options* is an approach that considers investment projects, such as research and development spending, project-asset evaluation, mergers and acquisitions in a similar way to how stock options are valued. A stock option allows a relatively small investment to be made today keeping open the possibility of making a bigger investment at a later date if the future goes according to plan. If it does not the investor can walk away. Proponents of this approach claim that it can lead to better project valuation, capital budgeting, and strategic planning and that where factors such as demand, technology changes and costs can vary widely, using real options allows managers to consider that uncertainty and how they might best react to it. The approach can vary from an options 'way of thinking' through to highly complex mathematical modelling.
- *Software packages*, which are available commercially, can be used as a tool to assist in the identification, analysis and documentation of risks.

Developing a
Risk Management Strategy

4.1 Defining the organisation's risk management strategy

Before strategies are developed for each of the risks identified in the risk mapping process, it is necessary to determine the organisation's attitude towards risk. Individuals have different attitudes to risk – some people tend to be risk averse and will try to avoid any possibility of uncertainty, whilst others are happy to take risks in the hope of higher returns. Profit may be seen as the reward for taking risks. Organisations also have different appetites for risk, which will determine the level of exposure to risk that is considered acceptable. This appetite for risk will influence the strategies that the organisation adopts for managing risks and the resource expended in doing so.

The risk appetite will be influenced by the size and type of the organisation, its capacity for risk and its ability to exploit opportunities and withstand setbacks. A large diversified organisation may be more able to withstand the impact of certain individual events, whilst the same event might be catastrophic for a small company. It will also depend on the organisation's structure and culture – for example a small business is more likely to be influenced by the risk appetite of the individuals running the business, who may be prepared to take risks. In addition, an organisation's ability to respond to events may differ, for example a small business can often make decisions more quickly as there are fewer formal processes. However, whatever the shape of the organisation, the strength of its resources, systems and processes will be a key factor in its capacity for risk; an organisation with a broad base of strengths will be best positioned to withstand the individual and cumulative effect of risks.

An organisation's environment can also influence its attitude to risk. For example, in a competitive environment an organisation, which is reluctant to take risks and is making low returns, may feel that it is actually more important to the long-term future of the business to pursue higher returns by taking greater risks and seizing opportunities.

To determine the organisation's appetite for risk it is necessary to consider a range of questions, such as:

- What is the organisation's current philosophy with regard to risk?
- What is the organisation's history of gains and losses?
- What is the expectation of investors and other stakeholders?

- What skills and experience do managers have?
- How strong is the organisation financially, including cash flow, balance sheet and debt position?

4.2 Choosing the right response to risks

Once the risks facing the business have been identified and assessed, and the organisation's appetite for risk determined, it is necessary to decide how best to respond to those risks. Just as there are many different types of risk, there will be a range of different approaches to managing them. The challenge to risk managers is finding the appropriate responses that combine to form a coherent, integrated strategy, such that the net remaining risk is within the acceptable level of exposure.

These responses may have differing aims, and may be designed to:

- Minimise the likelihood of an adverse event occurring.
- Maximise the likelihood of a positive outcome.
- Reduce the impact of a risk.

There is usually no right response – different organisations may make different decisions when facing the same risk. One may choose to leave a particularly risky business completely whilst another chooses to accept the risk but take action to mitigate it. There may also be more than one effect due to an individual risk, for example the potential financial loss may be acceptable whilst an associated impact on health and safety is not. Whatever the chosen response, it is important that adequate resource is allocated to the primary risk areas that relate to the core business of the organisation.

The choice of the appropriate response to a given risk will depend on a range of factors, including:

- The importance of the strategic objective to which the risk relates.
- The type of risk and whether it represents an opportunity or a threat.
- The direct and indirect impact of the risk.
- The likelihood of the risk.
- The cost of different responses to the risk.
- The organisation's environment.
- Constraints within the organisation.
- The organisation's ability to respond to events.

4.3 Possible responses to risk

Responses to risk generally fall into the following categories, each of which will be discussed in turn:

- risk retention;
- risk avoidance;
- risk reduction; and
- risk transfer.

4.3.1 Risk retention

Risk retention is a very common response to risks. Where no action is taken to avoid, reduce or transfer the risk, the possibility that the event will occur is accepted and the risk is retained. The captain (and hence the owners) of the Titanic retained the risk of collision with an iceberg by choosing to maintain a northerly route. Risk retention is not always deliberate; for example where a risk is not recognised, because there is no effective risk management, it will be retained by default. However in an organisation which has effective risk management it should be a positive decision taken because no other response was assessed as being more attractive or there is no other practical option.

Risks that are inherent in the organisation's activities are often accepted, particularly if they are reasonably predictable. In addition, organisations may decide to accept risks in order to seize opportunities which could lead to higher returns. Where risks are significant and retention is deliberate, it is important that this is clearly recognised, understood and agreed as part of the risk management strategy. If risks are retained because they are seen as insignificant, it is important that they are reviewed on a regular basis to ensure that they have not become more significant.

The level of risk which is retained is often referred to as 'residual' or 'net' risk.

4.3.2 Risk avoidance

Risks are avoided when an organisation chooses not to accept them and takes steps to avoid acting in a way that could cause the risk to happen. The Titanic, for example, could have avoided the risk presented by icebergs by sailing further south. However, a consequence of excessive or inappropriate use of risk avoidance is that an organisation may miss opportunities to make returns and may fail to achieve its objectives.

Strategies for risk avoidance generally involve the cessation of particular activities which have risks associated with them, such as manufacturing particular products or selling into specific markets. This may even involve selling parts of the business. It may also be possible to eliminate risk by changing or eliminating some of the organisation's processes.

4.3.3 Risk reduction

Risk reduction involves reducing, preventing or controlling the severity of loss from a potential occurrence (rather than preventing the occurrence itself as with risk avoidance). Examples of well-known risk reduction techniques include safety programmes, medical care and security systems. In the case of the Titanic, better lookouts could have reduced the risk of hitting the iceberg.

Preventing loss may appear to be the most desirable approach but in some cases complete prevention could cost more than the potential loss. Although it is not possible to prevent all losses, adequate preparation for responding to crises and other events will help reduce potential losses. For example, public relations departments play a key role in an organisation's response, as highlighted by the case of Perrier where further damage was caused due to the company's handling of events in the media. (see Chapter 1).

An organisation can also reduce its exposure to risk by diversifying into a range of different businesses or products. Whilst individual risks may carry large potential losses, the overall combined impact is not so great. On this basis bookmakers accept many individual exposures without facing the same overall possibility of loss themselves. Retail companies that use all possible means of selling goods are exposed to less overall risk than those who are selling through one distribution channel such as the internet.

> **An example of a risk reduction activity**
> **Business continuity planning**
>
> Much has been written about this subject recently, particularly in the wake of the events of 11 September 2001. Following the collapse of the World Trade Center, it was those organisations which had a robust business continuity plan who were able to respond to the crisis most effectively. Business continuity plans contain the organisation's response to unexpected and significant business interruptions, which can result from a range of different causes, such as fire, terrorist activities, power failure or computer viruses. One well-known example is the preparation of underground bunkers or other secure locations for governments to evacuate to in times of crisis.
>
> Business continuity plans should not just be about the short term, but about rebuilding the business in the aftermath of the event. A well-prepared plan for re-establishing critical business activities quickly and effectively can make the difference between the survival or complete loss of the business.

4.3.4 Risk transfer

The impact of risks can sometimes be reduced by transferring all or part of the risk to another individual or organisation that is more willing or able to bear the risk. Common examples of risk transfer are hedging and insurance. It is likely that White Star, the owners of the Titanic, insured the ship against loss. Certainly individuals on board insured their property and a wide range of claims were submitted. Risks may also be transferred through contracts in which one organisation assumes the possibility of loss from another. For example, risks relating to product liability may be transferred between manufacturers and retailers. It is interesting to note that the increasing importance of corporate risk management has led to the development of novel forms of insurance. The market now offers insurance to cover such events as the weather, business interruption and environmental damage.

If risks are transferred, it is important that the arrangements are explicit and clearly understood by both parties.

A risk transfer strategy
Integrated insurance policies

It is not unusual for large organisations to have many different insurance policies for individual risks, from different insurance providers and with different renewal dates – an administrative burden. However, over recent years there has been a move towards integrated insurance policies which are designed to cover a number of risks, often over several years, to avoid a continuous renewal process. These policies not only cover traditional risks, but also are beginning to include risks not previously covered (see the case study on United Grain Growers in Appendix 1). They can be customised to address the unique characteristics of the business, and can sometimes lead to different strategic decisions, as risks which would previously have been avoided can be transferred. Such policies can also lead to a decrease in the total cost of insurance premiums and a reduction in administration costs.

The use of such policies does not necessarily reduce other work – it is still necessary to consider individual risks and their impact, and managing such complex policies can be difficult. In-depth analysis of the various functions is required before such a policy can be developed. However, much of this will form part of the implementation of an integrated risk management programme. Integrated insurance policies take a long time to set up, but then release managers to focus on the remainder of the risk management process.

It is important to look at such policies alongside other methods of responding to risk as part of the organisation's overall strategy. These policies should complement, not replace other options, and are likely to be of most use where they incorporate previously uninsurable risks.

5

Implementing a
Risk Management Process

Once the risk management strategy has been developed, responsibilities should be allocated and the strategy communicated to those responsible for its implementation. For the plan to be effective it is essential that responsibility for each specific action be assigned to the appropriate operational manager and that clear target dates are established for each action. It is also important to obtain the co-operation of those responsible for the strategy, by formal communication, seminars, action plans, and adjustments to budgets.

5.1 Ensuring successful implementation

There are several key success factors for ensuring successful implementation of risk management in any organisation. These are outlined below.

5.1.1 Top-level commitment

There must be active commitment from the board to risk management to ensure that it is aligned with the organisation's objectives and integrated with the strategic planning processes. It is also important in encouraging support from the rest of the organisation. Securing the necessary commitment can sometimes be difficult but different approaches can be taken to persuade the board to take risk management seriously. For example, some will respond to reminders of the benefits to the organisation, whilst others will respond purely to statutory responsibility. It may be necessary to spend time understanding the driving concerns for each individual and responding accordingly.

5.1.2 Integration into strategic planning

As previously mentioned, integrated risk management is an important route to ensure improved performance. However, this can only be achieved if the risk management process is fully integrated with the strategic management of the organisation and risks are analysed and prioritised based on the organisation's overall objectives. One way of achieving this is to establish a series of points of comparison and feedback between the organisation's risk management and overall strategic management at key stages in the process.

5.1.3 Ownership and support within the organisation

Without support from all levels within the organisation, risk management will not be effective. Communication of the risk management strategy is key in achieving this. As suggested in Chapter 3, the involvement of staff in identifying and assessing risks will assist in establishing ownership, as well as increase awareness and understanding of the importance of risk management to the organisation's future.

5.1.4 Risk management as a continuous process

Risk management is not a one-off activity. The organisation will always face risks that will be continuously changing and evolving. The risk management process must regularly review those risks and develop strategies to respond. An organisation must learn from the experience of risk management and adapt and improve the process accordingly.

5.1.5 A supportive culture

The implementation of integrated risk management within an organisation will vary according to the culture of the organisation and may demand a different approach and behaviour from managers to staff. If no account is taken of the existing culture, the implementation will not succeed. If a change in culture is required, this can form the focus of training programmes and other activities to communicate changed values, but it may also be necessary to change the organisation or individual jobs, performance management systems, rewards and incentives.

5.1.6 A system embedded in the organisation's processes

Making risk management procedures part of the daily activities increases the likelihood that they will be carried out. Over time, these processes become more automatic and risk management becomes part of everyone's job. For example, in one company providing consultancy services, a new client account cannot be opened until a full 'know your customer' check has been carried out with acceptable results which are then documented.

5.1.7 Building on good practice and processes

Incorporating the risk management process into existing practices within the organisation will mean that it is more likely to be taken seriously rather than being seen as another new fad. In addition it will minimise the increase in administration by using current monitoring and reporting processes and is therefore more likely to receive support from staff. Implementation of a risk management strategy can sometimes even involve the elimination of processes.

5.1.8 A common language and framework throughout

Historically, risk management approaches have often been developed independently in different parts of the organisation. As a result, inter-relationships between business units and departments may be ignored, good practice is not always shared and the aggregate risks are not examined. Perceptions of risk may differ in different parts of the organisation. To avoid these problems, a common language and framework should be developed which includes a risk management policy, clear guidelines and reporting systems. This framework should also emphasise the risk of missing valuable opportunities.

5.1.9 Flexibility to accommodate different areas

Whilst a common framework and organisation-wide approach is essential, there must also be flexibility to allow for the fact that the same risk can affect different parts of the organisation in different ways.

5.1.10 A thorough and detailed identification process

The identification and assessment process must be comprehensive and cover all activities and levels in the organisation, including the activities of the board as well as front-line activities. However, it is important that the level of initial analysis is sufficient to identify key risks in a timely manner. These risks can then be analysed in more detail, without overloading the risk management process with data.

5.1.11 Taking into account the capacity for managing risks

An organisation as a whole can look at a large number of risks but there is a limit to the number which an individual manager or team can manage effectively without becoming overloaded. Some risks are managed more naturally at a certain level, but the capacity of those being asked to manage risks must also be taken into account.

Appendix 5 contains a checklist to help consider whether the implementation plan is comprehensive.

5.2 Roles and responsibilities

Whilst risk management must involve everyone in an organisation, particular responsibility will belong to certain groups or individuals. These responsibilities should be clearly documented.

5.2.1 The board

Overall responsibility for risk management must be at the highest level within the organisation. This will ensure that the strategy has authority and commitment from the top, and that the risk management group and officers responsible for implementing the strategy have the necessary support and resources at their disposal. In addition, the involvement of the senior management is critical if risk management is to be aligned with the strategic objectives of the organisation.

It is likely that the finance director or chief finance officer will be the individual who introduces risk management to the board, but it may be driven by anyone who is aware of and concerned about risks. For example, in healthcare organisations clinicians often drive risk management.

As the UK's Turnbull Committee (see Chapter 1: Why Manage Risk?) stated in its report, 'the board of directors is responsible for the company's system of internal control and should seek regular assurance that will enable it to satisfy itself that the system is functioning effectively. The board must further ensure that the system of internal control is effective in managing risks in the manner which it has approved.'

This responsibility includes:

- Reviewing the risks facing an organisation.
- Determining its appetite for risk.
- Monitoring the effectiveness of the risk management process, including receiving reports from line managers.
- Reviewing significant issues and any failures in the system.
- Communicating the policy throughout the organisation and gaining commitment to risk management.

5.2.2 Audit committee

If an Audit Committee exists within the organisation, it can carry out a key role in ensuring the effectiveness of risk management and internal control. Audit Committees should be composed of independent non-executive directors. There is an absolute need for probing and questioning with diligent follow up where required. Specifically, members of the Audit Committee must be questioning of both the management and the auditors, internal and external.

An effective Audit Committee will meet regularly with internal and external audit independently from the organisation's management. The Committee also decides the scope of internal audit in the context of risk management, monitors the performance of internal audit and ensures the reliability of financial reporting, key to effective risk management. To do this, members will need to be proactive, be aware of the issues facing the organisation, and understand the risk framework and context under which the organisation operates.

5.2.3 Risk management group

As described in Chapter 2, a risk management group may be established to facilitate and co-ordinate risk management across an organisation. This group would promote the understanding and assessment of risk, and facilitate the development of a strategy to deal with the identified risks.

The risk management group may be responsible for reviewing systems and procedures, identifying and assessing risks and introducing the controls that are best suited to the particular business unit.

Possible members of the group could include a chief risk officer, a non-executive director, finance director, internal auditor, heads of planning and sales, treasurer and operational staff.

5.2.4 Chief risk officer (risk manager)

Depending on its size, an organisation may appoint a full-time risk officer or allocate this responsibility to a senior manager. This individual will have responsibility for facilitating and co-ordinating all risk management activities, ensuring that all the risk management and monitoring functions work well together. The chief risk officer will also facilitate the co-operation between the various people and departments dealing with risk management and ensure that the necessary information is provided to the board and other parties.

5.2.5 Internal audit

Larger organisations may have an internal audit function providing objective assurance of the organisation's risk management and the internal control systems. Internal audit may provide an assessment of whether the organisation's risk management is adequate and effective, and may also perform an advisory function.

It is important that the internal audit programme is aligned with the risk management strategy. It is not uncommon for internal audit programmes to be developed to consider all parts of the business on a cyclical basis, but to enable effective risk management the internal audit programme should instead focus on controls relevant to key risks. There is a trend in some larger organisations to combine internal audit and risk management into one function.

The FMAC/CIMA theme booklet includes two articles on the changing role of internal audit.

5.2.6 External audit

External auditors of listed companies are required to review the directors' report on internal control and risk management. They may also perform independent assessment of the process, particularly in cases where internal audit has designed the process.

5.2.7 Line managers

Line managers will be responsible for risk management within their own departments. As part of the risk management strategy, actions to manage and monitor risks will be identified and will need to be carried out at a departmental level. Those responsible for allocating resources to different activities need to consider the risks involved in those activities when making their decisions.

Managers and their staff may also be involved in the risk identification and assessment process. Increased involvement at this stage is likely to lead to greater ownership of the whole process.

Should risk management be outsourced?

As risk management is rising up the agenda for all organisations, increasing numbers of businesses are offering services in risk-related areas. These range from companies offering support in particular areas of risk management such as loss adjusters (for claims-handling and support services) and business continuity specialists to independent risk consultants offering help with the whole process from development to implementation of the risk strategy.

Outsourcing the risk management function can offer advantages, particularly to small organisations or those taking the first steps towards integrated risk management. Specialist companies will have knowledge of the latest trends in identifying and responding to risks, as well as breadth of experience and an understanding of good practice. They may also have existing relationships with brokers and insurance companies. It may well prove more cost-effective to buy-in skills and technical support than to develop an in-house function.

However, in making a decision to outsource any part of the risk management function it must be remembered that whatever support is provided by consultants it is still the organisation itself which needs to manage the risks. It is essential to ensure that risk management is embedded in an organisation's culture. It is also important in any outsourcing exercise to ensure that the organisation retains control of any activities which contribute to the achievement of its strategic objectives, such as risk management. Consultants may provide technical support but the client organisation should be responsible for final decisions on the risk management strategy.

5.2.8 Individual employees

Individual employees are responsible for operating internal control processes as part of their role. This should form part of the account-ability for achieving their objectives. All employees also need to be aware of the risks that relate to their area of work.

An example of an organisation structure for risk management is contained in Appendix 6.

5.3 The risk management framework

Once the strategy has been defined and roles and responsibilities assigned, it must be communicated to the entire organisation. There are various means of communication available, and a framework should be developed to include a range of different mechanisms.

5.3.1 A risk management policy

The development and distribution of a risk management policy is key to communicating the overall strategy. It provides the context for the risk management activities and a framework for decision making. The policy outlines the rationale behind the development of risk manage-ment and the organisation's attitude to risk. The policy, which is a formal document approved by the board, will help by:

- Demonstrating senior management commitment.
- Clarifying the objectives of risk management.
- Defining roles and responsibilities.
- Describing the process.
- Outlining the reporting and review processes.

An example of a risk management policy can be found in Appendix 7.

5.3.2 Risk management guidelines

The more detailed description of the risk management strategy and processes should be included in risk management guidelines. These guidelines should document the entire process from the risk identifi-cation and analysis through to operational control processes and mon-itoring. Effective risk management guidelines will ensure everyone is aware of their own role and provide a basis for assurance. Guidelines enable the process by:

- Providing a means for sharing information about risk management.
- Facilitating the monitoring and review of risk management.
- Providing evidence to stakeholders of a systematic and thorough approach to risk management.
- Documenting risks.
- Documenting control processes.
- Providing a framework for accountability.

Guidelines for individual risk responses may also be developed as working documents, such as business continuity plans and the performance measurement system.

Appendices 7 and 8 contain example outlines of risk management guidelines and a business continuity plan.

5.3.3 Monitoring and reporting

The monitoring and reporting process should be formalised and documented. The purpose of the reporting process is to ensure that risk management is working effectively and is responding appropriately to the risks facing the organisation. The reports must be timely, straightforward to complete and form part of the regular reporting of the business. It is particularly important for large organisations to have a system to monitor the progress towards implementation of an integrated risk management strategy and the effectiveness of the risk management activities themselves.

Reports will need to be generated for different groups within the organisation, and they will have different requirements. Appendix 10 contains an example of an analysis of the needs of different users.

If risk management within the organisation is fully integrated, it should become part of the general reporting of the business rather than be reported on separately. In organisations where risk management is fully embedded in the systems, processes and culture, it can become incorporated in all aspects of reporting, for example as part of budget reviews and investment appraisal. Indeed, the inclusion of risk management issues in such processes and reports can help to reinforce risk management as an integral part of every activity.

Internal audit has an important role to play in providing independent assurance of the risk management process, in evaluating the control systems and their effectiveness. As previously mentioned, it is important that the internal audit programme is based on and integrated with the risk management process.

External reporting

There is increasing pressure on organisations to improve risk reporting to stakeholders outside the organisation, for example to shareholders through annual reports. As stated in CIMA's article on improved risk disclosure in the FMAC/CIMA theme booklet the focus over the last few years has been on ensuring an effective internal risk management framework. Now the focus is turning to how much organisations can tell investors about the outcomes of the risk management process. These demands have intensified in the wake of the Enron collapse and the resultant loss of confidence in corporate reporting. Companies are being asked to produce information that really demonstrates that the organisation has an effective risk management programme, particularly one that takes account of the 'softer', non-financial risks that are more difficult to quantify but are often a cause of failure. Additionally, there are likely to be requirements to improve reporting placed on companies by new requirements, such as the Operating and Financial Review proposed in the UK by the Company Law Review.

Currently, most organisations produce very little detail on risk management; most reporting is confined to statements that simply describe internal control procedures. Very few produce statements that demonstrate that there is an integrated process that is designed to ensure that the organisation meets its objectives. There may be several reasons why this information is not provided. It is often seen as too commercially sensitive, or open to misinterpretation. There may also be concerns that the information could be used against the organisation's managers if future events occur that were not foreseen. It may also be that the information is seen as too complex and difficult to convey.

However, demand for better information will continue, and organisations will have to consider how to meet the requirements of stakeholders and legislation. While there are issues to resolve, such as what to report and how to strike a balance between too much disclosure and too little, any organisation with a well-developed approach to risk management should be in a position to demonstrate its effectiveness and perhaps should be more transparent with the capital markets about the nature of business risks it faces. Some companies are already beginning to do so, and it is likely that others will need to follow.

5.3.4 Education and training

Some form of education and training is likely to form part of any risk management strategy, although its actual format will depend on the organisation's characteristics and needs, as well as the level and role of the individual staff being trained. The purpose of such a programme would be to raise awareness of what risk management is and educate staff in risk management policies and practice. An ongoing programme can also be used to facilitate and encourage involvement in the risk management process, provide a forum for feedback to managers and enable them to reinforce issues arising from the risk management process.

Appendices

APPENDIX 1

RISK MANAGEMENT IN ACTION –
THE CASE OF UNITED GRAIN GROWERS

United Grain Growers (UGG) of Winnipeg was one of the first corporations to change its risk management practices to reflect enterprise (or integrated) risk management. UGG provides commercial services to farmers, and markets agricultural products world-wide. With revenues of 209 million Canadian dollars in 1999, UGG was the third largest provider of grain handling services in western Canada, with about a 15 per cent market share. It was founded in 1906 as a farmer-owned cooperative and became a publicly-traded company in 1993, while retaining its cooperative roots. The company includes both members, generally farmers who do business with UGG, and shareholders.

Several factors led UGG to investigate enterprise risk management. The requirement of the Toronto Stock Exchange that boards of directors of listed corporations identify the corporation's principal risks and implement appropriate systems to manage them was one factor. Other factors included increased requirements to disclose exposure to risk; increased emphasis on risk management by credit rating agencies; and UGG's perception that the recommendations of equity analysts were sensitive to earnings results that deviated from those forecast. Although UGG hedged most of its currency and commodity price risk and purchased insurance against property and liability losses, its earnings continued to exhibit substantial volatility.

Identifying and assessing risk

UGG started by forming a risk management committee consisting of the CEO, CFO, risk manager, treasurer, compliance manager (for commodity trading), and the manager of corporate audit services. This committee, along with a number of UGG employees, then met with a representative from Willis Group Ltd., a major insurance broker, for a brainstorming session to identify and qualitatively rank the organisation's major risks. This process identified 47 exposure areas, from which the top six were chosen for further investigation and quantification.

The risks were:

* environmental liability;
* the effect of weather on grain volume;

- counterparty risk (suppliers or customers not fulfilling contracts);
- credit risk;
- commodity price and basis risk; and
- inventory risk (damage to products in inventory).

Willis Risk Solutions, a unit of the Willis Group Ltd., took on the task of gathering data and estimating the probability distribution of and correlations among losses from each of the six risk exposures. These probability distributions were then used to quantify the impact of each source of risk, both alone and in combination, and on several measures of UGG's performance, including return on equity, economic value added (EVA), and earnings before interest and taxes (EBIT). The analysis conducted by Willis Risk Solutions led to the conclusion that, of the six risks originally identified, UGG's main source of unmanaged risk was weather. Willis and UGG therefore focused their energies on understanding how weather affected UGG's performance. The analysis established a relationship between weather and UGG's gross profit by linking weather to crop yields, crop yields to grain volume, and grain volume to profit. Using these estimated relationships, Willis was able to show clearly the historic impact of weather on UGG's earnings volatility.

Managing the risk

UGG considered the following three options for managing its weather risk:

1. Maintain the status quo and retain exposure.
2. Hedge exposure using weather derivatives.
3. Use industry-wide grain shipment as the variable that would trigger payments from its insurers and integrate grain volume 'coverage' with traditional property and liability coverage.

Maintaining the status quo and simply retaining the exposure would subject earnings to large swings due to weather variation. Accepting this volatility had several disadvantages. First, UGG planned large investments in high-throughput grain elevators and since external capital would be needed, the rate that the organisation would have to pay on borrowed funds was likely to be higher if it retained the weather risk. Also, greater earnings volatility would prevent UGG from using more debt financing and therefore prevent it from gaining additional interest tax shields. In addition UGG tries to distinguish itself from its competitors by creating products with brand names and by providing ongoing services to customers. Stability in the organisation's cash flows would increase the likelihood of being able to capitalise on past investments in brand name products and customer service.

The disadvantages of risk retention led UGG to consider hedging its exposure using weather derivatives. In 1999 the weather derivatives market was beginning to emerge, with several dealers willing to take on weather-related risks. However, UGG's needs would require contracts designed specifically for UGG and the costs of hedging with derivatives were likely to be high and the contracts would be illiquid. In addition, basic risk due to unexplained variation still remained. After many months of analysing how weather affected UGG's profit, the CFO and risk manager considered an alternative approach. They reasoned that weather was important because it affected the amount of grain produced and therefore the amount of grain that UGG shipped. This suggested that a better solution would be to design a contract that directly reimbursed UGG when its grain shipments were lower than expected.

The problem with such a contract arises from the fact that grain shipments are in part a function of UGG's pricing and service. The solution was to use industry-wide grain shipment as the variable that would trigger payments to UGG. Industry shipments were highly correlated with UGG's shipments. In addition, relative to a contract based on weather, a contract based on grain shipments had the advantage of hedging against non-weather risks that might affect grain volume (such as regulatory policies and exchange rates). In addition, the relatively low market share meant that UGG's shipments would have minimal effect on the value of industry-wide shipments. As in the case of weather derivatives, a contract based on industry grain volume would have to be designed and priced – a costly process. One of the CFO's objectives was to manage the weather/grain volume exposure without substantially increasing the organisation's risk management costs.

UGG therefore considered integrating its grain volume 'coverage' with its other traditional property and liability coverage and eventually entered into an integrated policy contract with Swiss Re. According to the terms of the contract, if industry grain volume in a given year is lower than the average industry grain volume over the previous five-year period, a grain volume 'loss' occurs, and UGG-receives a payment from Swiss Re. The new policy has retentions based on aggregate property losses and aggregate liability losses and also incorporates coverage for grain volume losses. In addition, there is an annual aggregate limit and a term aggregate limit for all the coverage.

The benefits and lessons for the future

UGG managers continue to work on an enterprise approach to risk management. They view the insurance contract with Swiss Re as the initial step in an ongoing process. They continue to evaluate other exposures with an eye toward integrating coverage for those exposures into their insurance contracts. Despite its ongoing nature, UGG's initial foray into the enterprise risk management area has yielded several benefits. The insurance contract provided coverage for a risk that the organisation previously did not (and could not) hedge. By hedging this risk, UGG is more likely to have the internal funds necessary to carry out its capital expenditure plan and to establish itself as a leading intermediary between farmers and end users. It is also in a better position to borrow additional capital and to increase its debt-to-equity ratio, and thereby benefit from additional tax shields. The integration of the organisation's insurance coverage with the grain volume coverage allowed the organisation to rearrange its overall coverage and keep its cost of risk roughly constant.

In addition, UGG's managers clearly indicate that they found the risk identification and measurement process highly valuable in itself. The managers feel that the process has given them a better understanding of the organisation's risks and that communication within the organisation about such risk exposures has improved.

Discussions with UGG's managers indicate that an enterprise risk management approach requires cooperation from many individuals across the organisation. To achieve this cooperation, top managers must 'buy in' to the idea and demonstrate their support. Enterprise risk management can also take time and patience to implement. UGG invested over three years from the initial brainstorming session to the signing the insurance contract. To be sure, subsequent enterprise risk management endeavours undertaken by Willis have taken considerably less time (approx. six to twelve months), but the need for top level 'buy-in' and organisation-wide cooperation remains unchanged.

Technical expertise is also important. Someone must estimate the probability distributions of various exposures and the correlation between them, as wells as quantify the impact of exposure on the organisation's results. Although consultants and brokers can provide the complex statistical and actuarial analyses, internal managers must be knowledgeable enough to provide input and to interpret the output. Nonetheless, the approach underlying UGG's grain volume coverage is likely to be applicable to other organisations.

Based on material from Harrington, S E; Niehaus, G and Risko, K J (Winter 2002), 'Enterprise Risk Management: the case of United Grain Growers', *Journal of Applied Corporate Finance*, pp. 71–81, Stern Stewart & Co, New York.

APPENDIX 2

STAGES IN THE DEVELOPMENT OF RISK MANAGEMENT

Adapted from *Risk Management: A Guide to Good Practice for Higher Education Institutions*, Higher Education Funding Council for England (HEFCE) 2001.

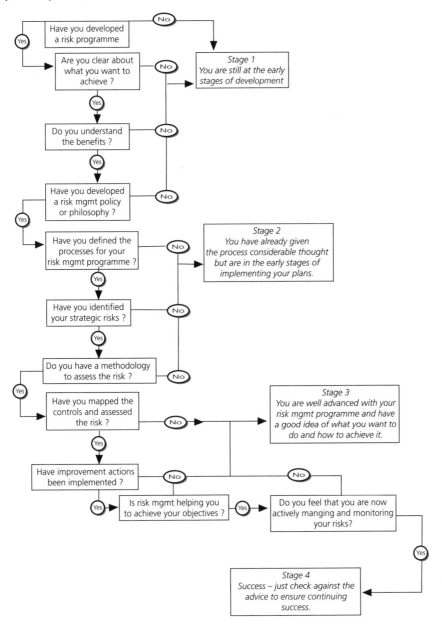

APPENDIX 3

EXAMPLE OF RISK ANALYSIS FOR A TELECOMMUNICATIONS COMPANY

Reproduced from Shimpi, P and Swiss Re New Markets, (1999 and 2001), *Integrating Corporate Risk Management*, Texere LLC, New York.

Operational risk

Operational control risk
Errors and omissions
Cost structure
Control procedures
Rebates and withdrawals
Governance and accountability

Employee relations risk
Human resources procedures
Industrial actions
Workers' compensation
Skills and training
Cultural mix

Information system risk
System synchronisation
Unauthorised system changes
Billing accuracy
Disaster recovery
Outsourced services

Network risk
Capacity & utilisation
Network fraud
Broadband utilisation
Network bottlenecks
Unplanned outages

Business risk

Business event risk
Technological advance
Regulatory change
Spectrum auction
Reputation damage
Business interruption

Service alliance risk
Service provider concentration
Alliance management
Outsourcing selection
Service quality
Service outages

Credit risk
Credit rating
Customer churn
Service provider liquidity
Trade credit
Political risk

Legal risk
Professional liability
Directors' and officers' liability
Contractual liability
Product liability
Third-party liability

Market risk

Equity risk
Shareholder management
Equity base
Dividend policy
Strategic investments
Capital expenditures

Product risk
Product complexity
Product obsolescence
Product development
Wholesale and retail mix
Packaging and delivery

Financial risk
Interest rates
Foreign exchange
Credit spreads
Tax expenditures
Cash flow and liquidity

Competitor risk
Pricing strategy
Market share
Churn management
Marketing strategy
Product array

APPENDIX 4

EXAMPLE OF A RISK MAP

Reproduced from Shimpi, P and Swiss Re New Markets, (1999 and 2001), *Integrating Corporate Risk Management*, Texere LLC, New York.

Risk profile of a pharmaceutical company

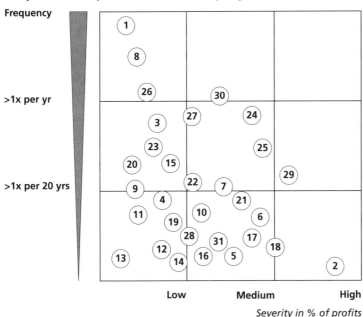

Severity in % of profits

Third party liability
1. Automobile liability/ aircraft
2. Product liability
3. Clinical trials
4. Premises liability
5. Fiduciary
6. Environment impairment (pollution)
7. Patent infringement

Workforce
8. Workers' compensation
9. Employers liability
10. D&O liability
11. EPL
12. Key person loss
13. Employee theft/dishonesty

Terrorism
14. Malicious tampering/ extortion
15. Theft/kidnapping/ bombing, etc.

First party damage/BI
16. Fire/explosion, etc.
17. Natural catastrophes
18. Business interruption
19. Machinery breakdown
20. Marine/cargo
21. Product recall
22. Data loss/ inaccuracy

Financial
23. Credit risk
24. Currency exchange rates
25. R&D investments
26. Interest rates
27. Negative publicity
28. Pension fund

Regulatory
29. FDA: mandated recall/ interr. in prod.
30. FDA: registration failures/delays

Political
31. Political risk, war

APPENDIX 5

IMPLEMENTATION PLAN – SELF-ASSESSMENT QUESTIONS

Adapted from *Risk Management: A Guide to Good Practice for Higher Education Institutions*, Higher Education Funding Council for England (HEFCE), 2001.

Once organisations have developed their plan for implementing a risk management programme, they may find it helpful to assess it against the following questions.

Objectives of the risk management programme

- Are there clear objectives for the programme?
- Do the objectives cover regulatory, strategic and operational requirements?
- What benefits do we expect and how will we assess if they are achieved?
- What are the anticipated benefits for different parties such as shareholders, customers and staff?

Management support

- Is the Chief Executive Officer supporting and sponsoring the process?
- Has the Board given approval to the process?
- Is there a high-level document such as a risk management policy that, once approved, gives authority to the process and outlines the responsibilities of different parties?
- How will managers and other staff be encouraged to support and participate?

Scope of the programme

- How wide-ranging should the process be?
- Do we have sufficient resources (finances and people) to implement everything at once?
- Would a staged implementation enable us to learn and evaluate along the way?
- How long will it take?

Embedding the process

- How is risk management linked with existing processes?
- How is the link being established between risk management, business planning and budget allocation?
- How is risk management linked to the organisation's strategic objectives?
- What role will internal audit play in risk management?
- How will risk management link to quality assessments?
- Does risk management need a separate reporting process?

Techniques for identifying risk

- What is the most effective and efficient way of identifying risk?
- How many risks should be considered?
- Who should be involved in the identification?
- How should we structure and prioritise the risks?

Risk assessment

- Who should be involved?
- Will everyone understand the risks?
- How should the assessment be done?
- Should there be confidentiality and anonymity?
- What is the right level of exposure?

Generating action

- What happens to the risks assessed as unacceptable?
- Will funding be available to address these risks?
- Who will ensure that action is taken to address these risks?

Reporting format

- How will the information be handled?
- What documentary evidence is required to support our disclosures?
- Who will information be reported to?
- Who will need access to the information?

Sustainability and flexibility of the process

- How do we ensure that the process keeps going?
- Do we need a risk manager or risk management committee?
- What should be the frequency and interval of the exercise?
- How do we measure the success of the process?
- How will changes to the process be implemented?
- How will the process be developed based on experience?

APPENDIX 6

EXAMPLE OF A RISK MANAGEMENT STRUCTURE
(from an international aid organisation)

Responsibilities and actions

Senior management

- Define the organisation's risk policy (organisational attitude to risk).
- Set-up risk management team drawn from core areas within the organisation.
- Determine terms of reference of the risk management team.

Risk management team (working with senior management)

- Identify the major risks facing the charity (threats to achieving objectives).
- Assess identified risks (evaluate potential impact).
- Review current strategies in place - draw up action plans if inadequate.
- Identify risk owners and agree action plans.
- Prepare risk management framework and risk register.
- Review implementation of action plans with risk owners.

Internal audit

- Incorporate risk management into audit programmes.
- Maintain the risk register.
- Report on risk management to senior management and audit committee.

Board of trustees

- Approve risk management framework.
- Report in annual report and accounts that risks have been assessed and are being appropriately managed in line with Statement of Recommended Practice (SORP) 2000.
- Validate risks on an annual basis.

APPENDIX 7

SAMPLE RISK MANAGEMENT POLICY

The following is an example of a policy that can be modified for use by any organisation

Background

This organisation has a commitment to the highest levels of performance and legal, ethical and moral standards. All members of staff are expected to share this commitment. This policy is established to facilitate the management of risk and enable enhanced business performance that is achieved without detriment to customers, staff or the environment.

This document, together with the Risk Management Guidelines, are intended to provide direction and help all officers, directors and staff with responsibility for managing risks. These documents provide a framework for the processes needed to identify, assess and respond to risks.

Risk management policy

It is the organisation's policy that in order to achieve high levels of performance it is necessary to undertake activities that involve a level of risk. However, the organisation will ensure that the decision processes regarding the response to risk are robust, open and clear.

It is the view of this organisation that risks are inherent in every activity undertaken. Therefore risk management is part of everyone's job.

The board's policy

The board will take overall responsibility for the development and implementation of the risk management strategy in accordance with this policy.

The board is committed to creating a culture where risk management is seen as a core activity that makes a positive contribution to the performance of the organisation.

The board is committed to maintaining clear and open discussions about its approach to risk management both within and the organisation and with other interested parties.

The board will support the risk management strategy by ensuring that necessary resources are in place for effective implementation; that processes are well documented and regularly reviewed; and that all staff understand and are equipped to carry out their roles.

APPENDIX 8

SAMPLE RISK MANAGEMENT GUIDELINES

1. Purpose of the guidelines

2. Risk management policy

3. The definition of risk

- The organisation's attitude to risk

4. Roles and responsibilities

- The board
- Audit committee
- Risk management group
- Chief risk officer
- Internal audit
- External audit
- Human resources
- Public relations
- Line managers
- All staff

5. Risk identification and analysis

- Description of the process
- Categories of risk
- Risk register for each risk:
  — Source of the risk
  — Nature of the risk
  — Impact and likelihood
  — Controls
  — Early warning indicators
- Testing and monitoring of controls

6. Organisation's response to risk

- Links to the business plan and objectives
- Response schedule and action plan
- Public communications policy
- Other supporting guidelines

7. Monitoring and review

- Regular internal monitoring
- External monitoring
- Review process

APPENDIX 9

SAMPLE BUSINESS CONTINUITY PLAN

1. Objectives of the plan

2. Roles and responsibilities

- Emergency response team
- Support teams:
  - Damage assessment
  - Salvage
  - Transportation team
  - Public information team
  - Telecommunications team
- The board
- Human resources
- Public relations
- Line managers
- All staff

3. Activating the plan

- By whom?
- On whose authority?

4. Task list

- Emergency response
  - Damage assessment
  - Notification procedures
  - Initiation of plan
  - Public communications
- Recovery plan

5. Communications

- Who needs to be informed?
- Key contacts
- Key messages

6. Priority for restoration of functions
(Staff, premises, systems)

- Critical functions
- Essential functions
- Necessary functions
- Desirable functions

7. Maintaining plan

8. Testing plan

9. Other information

- Suppliers' details
- Procedures for contacting suppliers
- Details of contracts

APPENDIX 10

ANALYSIS OF INFORMATION NEEDS FOR RISK MANAGEMENT

Adapoted from: IFAC and PricewaterhouseCoopers (1999), *Enhancing Shareholder Wealth by Better Managing Business Risk*, International Federation of Accountants.

Board of directors and business group reporting

User needs	Suggested response
The board of directors and most senior management need to:	
Know about the most significant exposure for the organisation.	Report on the top ten (or more) risks for the organisation and the major business groups including consolidated and sum-marised data.
Gain comfort that the business risk mgmt process is operating effectively.	Ensure the capacity to report on emerg-ing risks and other exceptional informa-tion and balanced status reporting (opportunities and hazards).
Gain an understanding of the sharehold-er value at risk, particularly within the control of management.	Impact measured in shareholder value terms with an indication of which risks are controllable through management action.
Analyse the trends of exposure.	Carry out year-on-year comparisons.
Be assured of the implementation of an appropriate, effective management response.	Design a questionnaire for the board of directors using a software-based assurance gathering process to establish the appropriate response to risk manage-ment.

Business unit reporting

User needs	Suggested response
Information about significant business risks under span of responsibility.	Matrix reporting by major area of business risk.
An indication of possible quick wins in risk response implementation.	Management's relative control over the risk response assessed.
Assurance that business risk management processes are operating effectively.	Information for significant business risk drivers are analysed and documented in database.
Sufficient data to monitor and assess business risk management performance of functional reports appropriately.	Reporting by accountable manager.
Assurance that appropriate management actions are being undertaken to enable sign-off of the board of directors' questionnaire.	Matrices provide information for active review process of key risks and performance of functional reports.
Renewable process to support continuous improvement.	Movement in risks over time reflected in risk profile matrices.

Individual reporting

User needs	Suggested response
Context and framework for understanding business risk and management business risk response.	All relevant data about risks contained in the business risk database including risk management action plan.
Information about risk drivers to monitor changes in risk intensity.	Risk drivers are analysed and documented.
Ownership of individual risks and understanding business risk management responsibilities.	Accountabilities determined.
Understanding the context of risk to enable continuous improvement of risk response.	Context and significance of risk established.

APPENDIX 11

SOURCES OF FURTHER INFORMATION

References and useful reading

CIMA Publications

- CIMA (2000), *Corporate Governance – History, Practice and Future.*
- CIMA (2001), *Fraud Risk Management – A Guide to Good Practice.*
- CIMA (2002), *Business Transparency in a Post-Enron World.*
- Fisher, C and Lovell, A (2000), *Accountants Responses to Ethical Issues at Work*, CIMA.
- CIMA/FMAC (2002), *Managing Risk to Enhance Stakeholder Value.*

Other publications

- AIRMIC, ALARM, IRM (2002), *A Risk Management Standard.*
- CBI and KPMG (2001), *Managing Business Risk*, Caspian Publishing and KPMG.
- Dembo, R and Freeman, A (1998) *Seeing Tomorrow – Rewriting the Rules of Risk*, John Wiley and Sons, Inc.
- Economist Intelligence Unit and MMC Enterprise Risk, Inc., (2001), *Enterprise Risk Management: Implementing New Solutions.*
- Financial Times (2000), *Mastering Risk* (ten-part series).
- HM Treasury (1997), *Managing the Risk of Fraud.*
- Higher Education Funding Council for England (2001), *Risk Management: A Guide to Good Practice for Higher Education Institutions.*
- ICAEW (1999), *Internal Control: Guidance for Directors on the Combined Code* ('The Turnbull Report').
- ICAEW (1999), No Surprises – T*he Case for Better Risk Reporting.*
- IFAC and PricewaterhouseCoopers (1999), *Enhancing Shareholder Wealth by Better Managing Business Risk*, International Federation of Accountants.
- Institute of Internal Auditors, UK and Ireland (1999), *Effective Governance.*
- McKinsey & Company (2002) *Global Investor Opinion Survey on Corporate Governance.*
- Scott E. Harrington, Greg Niehaus and Kenneth J. Risko, (Winter 2002), 'Enterprise Risk Management: the case of United Grain Growers', *Journal of Applied Corporate Finance*, pp. 71-81. [PUBLISHER AND PLACE?]
- Shimpi, P and Swiss Re New Markets, (1999 and 2001), *Integrating Corporate Risk Management*, Texere LLC, New York.

- Standards Association of Australia (1999), *AS/NZS 4360:1999, Risk Management.*
- Vaughan, E J (1997) *Risk Management*, John Wiley and Sons, Inc.

Websites

- CFO Europe:
    www.cfoeurope.com
- European Corporate Governance Institute:
    www.ecgi.org
- Higher Education Funding Council for England:
    www.hefce.ac.uk
- Independent Director:
    www.independentdirector.co.uk/reference.htm
- International Corporate Governance Network:
    www.icgn.org
- International Federation of Accountants:
    www.ifac.org
- International Risk Management Institute:
    www.irmi.com
- Risk Analysis and Management for Projects:
    www.ramprisk.com
- Risk Management Magazine:
    www.rmmag.com
- The Association of Insurance and Risk Managers, UK:
    www.airmic.com
- The Audit Commission, UK:
    www.audit-commission.gov.uk
- The Business Continuity Institute, UK:
    www.thebci.org
- The Institute of Risk Management, UK:
    www.theirm.org
- The Institute of Internal Auditors, UK and Ireland:
    www.iia.org.uk
- The Institute of Internal Auditors, Inc (US):
    www.theiia.org
- The National Forum for Risk Management in the Public Sector:
    www.alarm-uk.com

CIMA Technical publications

CIMA publishes a wide range of technical publications:
For more information contact:

CIMA Publishing
Publishing Sales Department
26 Chapter Street
London SW1P 4NP

Tel: 020 8849 2229/2277/2270
Fax: 020 8849 2465
E-mail: publishing-sales@cimaglobal.com

Or visit the CIMA website: www.cimaglobal.com

Index

Index

Risk Management – A Guide to Good Practice

NB: page numbers in italics indicate figures or tables